CAPTURED HISTORY

FIRST LOOK AT A BLACK HOLE

HOW A PHOTOGRAPH SOLVED A SPACE MYSTERY

by Danielle Smith-Llera

Consultant: Frank Summers, PhD
Space Telescope Science Institute

COMPASS POINT BOOKS
a capstone imprint

Captured History is published by Compass Point Books, an imprint of Capstone.
1710 Roe Crest Drive
North Mankato, Minnesota 56003
www.capstonepub.com

Library of Congress Cataloging-in-Publication Data is available on the Library of Congress website.
ISBN: 978-0-7565-6614-2 (library binding)
ISBN: 978-0-7565-6658-6 (paperback)
ISBN: 978-0-7565-6622-7 (ebook PDF)

Summary: On-point historical photographs combined with strong narration bring the story of the first photograph of a black hole to life. Kids will learn why it was so hard to take a photo of something so dark it does not reflect light, and so far away it could barely be reached. Primary source quotations bring the amazing accomplishment to life.

Image Credits
Alamy: The Picture Art Collection, 17, 54 (top); Courtesy of the Event Horizon Telescope Collaboration: 5; ESO: Event Horizon Telescope Collaboration, cover, 14, 57 (bottom right); Getty Images: AFP/Andrew Caballero-Reynolds, 51, Bettmann, 19, 22, 55; iStockphoto: elgol, 32; LIGO: SXS Project, 28, 56 (bottom); NASA: 31, 46, CXC/SAO, 25, 54 (bottom), ESA/F. Duccio Machetto, 27, 57 (top), ESA/G. Brammer, 6, Goddard Space Flight Center, 9, JPL-Caltech, 36, JPL-Caltech/IPAC/Event Horizon Telescope Collaboration, 52, M. Weiss (Chandra X-ray Center), 48; Newscom: Reuters/ Jeenah Moon, 45, Xinhua News Agency/Liu Jie, 38; Shutterstock: Chr. Offenberg, 35, 57 (bottom left), David Fowler, 56 (top), Manamana, 8, Mesa Studios, 11, Triff, 41; Wikimedia: Jean-Pierre Luminet, 20, Quentin Douchet, 50

Editorial Credits
Editor: Michelle Bisson; Designer: Tracy McCabe; Media Researcher: Svetlana Zhurkin; Production Specialist: Kathy McColley

Consultant Credits
Frank Summers, PhD, Space Telescope Science Institute

All internet sites appearing in back matter were available and accurate when this book was sent to press.

Printed in the United States 5273

TABLEOFCONTENTS

Chapter One

MONSTERS IN THE DARK

The astronomers anxiously watched weather forecasts displayed on a large monitor. It was about two o'clock in the afternoon on April 4, 2017, and this was the command center for the Event Horizon Telescope. Astronomer and project director Shep Doeleman sat at the conference table. His team hoped to capture the first image of a black hole in space, but the weather had to cooperate. In locations around the world, more than 200 people were waiting to switch on the largest telescope ever assembled.

Moisture of any kind can disturb the tiny waves of light arriving from light-years away. They are about 1 millimeter in length—short enough to get knocked off course by raindrops or even water vapor in clouds. Decades of work depended on the weather. But it wasn't the weather in their Cambridge, Massachusetts, room that afternoon that mattered.

At observatories in eight locations in the U.S., Mexico, Chile, Spain, and Antarctica, teams waited for Doeleman's online instructions to turn on their telescopes. When they did, the array would aim antennas, each cupped inside a parabolic dish, at the same point in the sky. The array of telescopes was called Event Horizon Telescope (EHT). Each telescope would gather data about the same target.

Shep Doeleman and his team members monitored the progress of the Event Horizon Telescope in locations around the world.

When combined, the data should make an image. Doeleman and his team hoped it would be the world's first photograph of a black hole—or whatever strange object they found instead.

The EHT's targets were located at the swirling centers of two galaxies. These objects had names, though no one had ever seen them. Sagittarius A* is about 25 million light-years away, inside our own spiral-shaped Milky Way galaxy. The other object is called M87*. It is tucked inside the oval-shaped Messier 87 (M87) galaxy, 53 million light-years away.

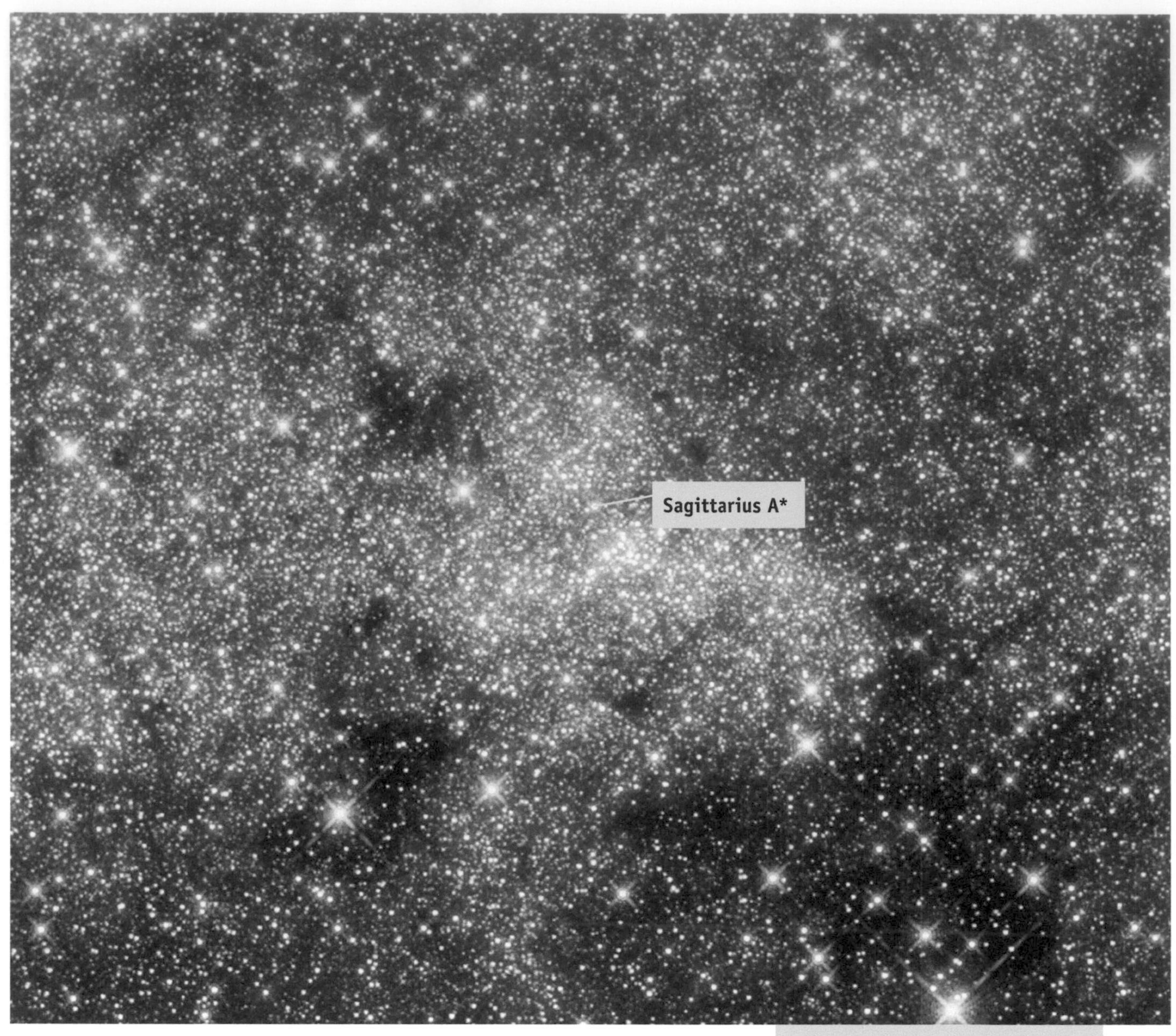

Though scientists have seen stars spinning around Sagittarius A*—located in the center of this image, taken with the Hubble Space Telescope—no one has ever seen the black hole itself.

M87 is so big and bright it was discovered in 1781 with an optical telescope. However, the EHT was not an optical telescope. Visible light is useless for hunting black holes. The EHT was a radio telescope that used light not visible to humans.

But unlike a normal shadow, a black hole has mass—great mass, in fact.

Even without a photograph, scientists could already picture a black hole. They imagined a dark sphere. It has no surface, like a shadow. But unlike a normal shadow, a black hole has mass—great mass, in fact. Like the sun or any star with great mass, a black hole pulls matter into its orbit. But a black hole's mass and gravity are greater than any other known object in the universe. Anything in its orbit that slips too close—dust, clouds of gas, stars—can break apart and spiral inward toward its center. Even light cannot escape a black hole. Scientists named the black hole's edge—the boundary where matter and light disappear—the event horizon.

How can anyone take a photograph of a black object against the darkness of space? A light source is necessary. That's true for any sort of photography. Fortunately, a black hole of a certain size can create a ring of light. Matter outside the event horizon whips around up to 2 million miles per hour (3.2 million kilometers/hour). This swirling belt is called an accretion disk. Its motion and magnetic fields agitate electrons that create radio waves—a form of light. That's why the EHT is a radio telescope. If the EHT were able to detect enough radio waves, its team members could turn them into a photograph. They knew how it would probably look. The accretion disk would look like a glowing ring. The black hole would appear as a shadow framed inside.

RADIO VISION

The 28 radio telescopes of the Very Large Array in New Mexico help scientists study faraway astronomical objects, including black holes.

The EHT may not look like a camera, but to take a black hole photograph it must do everything a regular camera does. Photographers working with dim visible light must keep the camera's shutter open longer to collect enough light bouncing off their subjects. Radio astronomers must observe dim targets for a long time too. Since radio waves carry very little energy compared to visible light, radio telescopes must be large, even as much as 1,640 feet (500 meters) wide. The EHT's fuzzy image would be crisper if the EHT had been larger. Its baseline, or distance between telescopes, would need to be larger than Earth.

A clean, high-quality lens gives a camera its viewing power. The polished surface inside a parabolic dish gives a radio telescope its viewing power. Even tiny bumps or scratches on the polished metal tiles inside a parabolic dish can disrupt radio waves. They must bounce off these mirrors toward a central antenna. The radio waves are converted into electricity and travel through cables to the control room. There, the electricity is recorded in sequences of numbers as digital information.

Like cameras, radio telescopes must aim at their subjects. The equipment that moves a radio telescope is complex and expensive. But without it, the polished dish cannot bounce radio waves at the antennas with accuracy. Machines swivel and tilt the dish to adjust its position. Computer-controlled machines also adjust the angle of each mirrored tile inside the dish.

This is a NASA artist's rendering of star debris gathered into an accretion disk around a black hole.

A black hole is so far away that the accretion disk appears as tiny as an orange resting on the moon, viewed from Earth. The most powerful optical telescope on Earth could focus on the moon's surface—but that area would be large enough to hold 20 billion oranges. To photograph such a distant and dim object would require a radio telescope—one as large as Earth itself. Such a telescope was impossible to build. However, an array of radio telescopes arranged over a large area could function like an enormous telescope. "Imagine taking a hammer, smashing a radio dish, and spreading the fragments all over the Earth," Doeleman later said. "In reality, we did that by linking up telescopes on different continents." This 50-year-old technique is called Very Long Baseline Interferometry (VLBI). Scientists can create a single image by combining data gathered from the array of telescopes. The EHT's 79 dishes at eight locations spread across three continents was the world's largest VLBI experiment.

But so much can go wrong with VLBI. Clouds in Arizona could creep near Mount Graham's observatory. Snow that had been forecasted for Mexico's Sierra Negra mountains could make trouble for an observatory there. But Doeleman's team could not afford to be too picky about conditions. Scheduling time on all eight observatories required negotiation and patience. Other astronomers used these sophisticated tools also. And weather conditions were clear at the observatories in Chile's Atacama Desert, California's Inyo Mountains, Spain's Sierra Nevada mountains, and on Hawaii's Mauna Kea.

"I think we should call it a go," Doeleman announced to the room. On a laptop, he typed a message into a private online chat used by the teams at the eight EHT observatories: "GO for VLBI. . . . This is NOT a drill."

Doeleman asked a teammate for a dramatic countdown. "Five. Four. Three. Two. One. All right, things should be recording," said EHT researcher and engineer Jason SooHoo. It was 6:31 p.m. Eastern Standard Time and the quiet, long work of radio astronomy had begun. When interferometry works correctly, the telescopes move in sync on preprogrammed tracks, following identical targets.

The EHT design turned Earth into a giant disco ball scattered with mirrors. As Earth turned, each of the array's mirrored dishes would collect light to combine into a photograph.

The EHT arrays spun into position one after the other. First, Spain's dish rolled into position to fix on a distant target. As Earth rotated, its instruments captured many angles of each target and recorded the information. After a few hours, the next telescopes rolled into position to begin observing the same target: Mexico's dish and, in Chile, another dish, along with a giant array of 66 dishes. Next, a dish in Arizona and an array of 23 dishes in California slid into position.

The telescope at the South Pole was one of many dishes around the world that kept watch on the black holes Shep Doeleman hoped to finally photograph.

Hours later, another telescope with an array of eight dishes in Hawaii took over the observation work. All the while, yet another dish at the South Pole—though it had technical problems that first observation day—kept steady watch on the distant target.

For more than a week, each day at EHT headquarters in Cambridge began with nervous phone calls to EHT locations around the world. The team analyzed weather data and checked whether the telescopes were ready for another day of observation. Turning on the EHT if the weather or telescope technology was not cooperating was a waste of time and money.

But good luck was in the forecast for the EHT. Doeleman was grateful for "an astonishing spate of planet-wide good weather." In fact, the clear weather meant research teams at the observatories had little time to rest. For half of the next 10 days, observatory teams stayed up all night watching over equipment and the weather. They grabbed naps during the day and spent sleepless nights overseeing delicate equipment. When the telescopes stopped tracking without explanation or had trouble focusing, the teams had to rush to reboot and repair.

The morning the EHT finished its last scan—April 11—was unforgettable for Doeleman. He said later, "You really feel that you are going to see something that is new, and that no one else has seen before."

"You really feel that you are going to see something that is new, and that no one else has seen before."

In 2012, the EHT had tried to photograph M87*. But it did not have enough high-quality data to make a clear image. Would the EHT succeed this time?

Waiting for an answer would take patience. VLBI does not produce quick snapshots. During the observation "we basically had to freeze light onto these hard drives," explained EHT computer specialist Katie Bouman. Team members would not see an image of the source of that light for more than a year. Putting all that data together required complex math, logic, and the help of computers.

The EHT recorded an enormous amount of data: five petabytes. That's about equal to "the entire selfie collection over a lifetime of 40,000 people," EHT astronomer Dan Marrone later said. But as observatory teams packed up their hard drives into foam crates, they had no idea whether the data would be useful for making an image. They drove the hard drives down mountain roads to ship them to EHT team members who would find out what was on them. Harsh winter weather in the southern hemisphere delayed the South Pole's data from arriving by eight months. More than 1,000 hard drives from around the world arrived at the MIT Haystack Observatory in Westford, Massachusetts, and at the Max Planck Institute for Radio Astronomy in Bonn, Germany.

It took a month of analyzing the data for the EHT members to hear good news. Researchers reviewing the data noticed similarities in the data from the observatories. These were clues that the array of telescopes had worked together as one eye and had seen *something* inside both galaxies. EHT members promised to keep their progress secret. They didn't want to disappoint the public if they failed. And if they succeeded, they didn't want to give away the surprise too soon.

Was it a bagel? A cat's eye? Pasta? Nope. It was the first image of M87*.

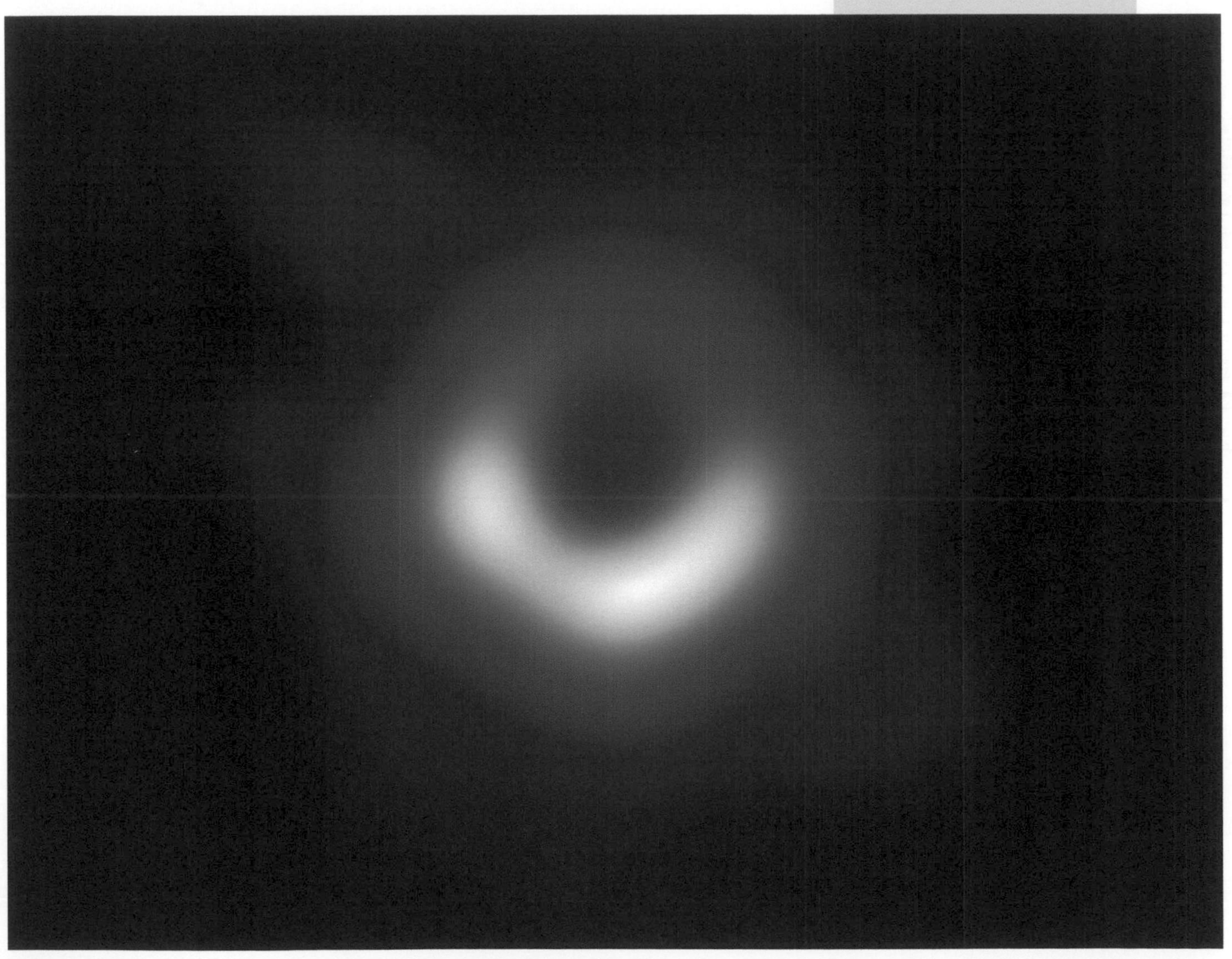

Finally, on April 10, 2019, a day short of two years since the EHT turned its dishes toward Sagittarius A* and M87*, the team presented a photograph to the world. To the public, the image of the M87* black hole was vivid—and a bit confusing. It reminded some of a cat's eye. Others thought it looked like a bagel or a piece of tortellini pasta floating in a dark soup. But to black hole experts like Doeleman, the image was miraculous. At a press conference in Washington, D.C., that day, Doeleman stated, "We have seen what we thought was unseeable."

Chapter Two

SMALL CLUES, BIG IDEAS

"We've been studying black holes so long that sometimes it's easy to forget that none of us has actually seen one," said France Córdova, the director of the National Science Foundation, on the day they finally did. But well before the Event Horizon Telescope's photograph changed that, even centuries ago, scientists had imagined their existence.

In 1783, British scientist John Mitchell envisioned strange objects in space that radiate no light. His theory was based on a law of gravity introduced by Isaac Newton a century earlier. The law stated that the greater an object's mass, the stronger its power to pull other matter toward it. Large objects in space create strong gravity. Earth creates gravity we can feel, for example. Since the sun contains 1 million times more mass than Earth, its gravity keeps the entire solar system in its orbit. But what if a star is so massive that even light cannot escape its gravity? Mitchell calculated how a star like the sun could become a "dark star." The sun—almost 865,000 miles (1.4 million km) wide—would need to be crushed into a supermassive object just a few miles across.

More than a century later, a new theory of gravity explained why such light-trapping objects could exist.

German astronomer Karl Schwarzschild used Einstein's equations to figure out how a black hole would trap light.

In 1915, German physicist Albert Einstein proposed that the extreme gravity of highly dense objects can bend space—and even time—a bit like how a bowling ball resting on a trampoline stretches the fabric. In 1916, German astronomer Karl Schwarzschild used Einstein's new equations to calculate how an object could trap light. How dense would it need to be?

Schwarzschild's calculations showed how mass compressed into a relatively tiny space could become a black hole—such as a star with 10 times the mass of the sun that is crushed into a sphere with the diameter of New York City—about 305 square miles (490 square km). Any mass can become a black hole if it's packed tightly enough. The sun compressed to a radius of 1.5 miles (2.4 km) would trap all matter and light. Earth compressed to a radius of 0.4 inches (1 centimeter)—not much larger than a pencil eraser—would too. Even a large mountain would become a black hole if compressed to a radius of less than a billionth of a meter. "If you took a baseball and crushed it down small enough, eventually it would rip the fabric of space-time too," said Caltech physicist Fiona Harrison.

"If you took a baseball and crushed it down small enough, eventually it would rip the fabric of space-time too."

How—in real life—does a supermassive object get pressed into an area so small? In the 1930s, a 19-year-old astrophysicist born in what is now Pakistan helped answer that question. Subrahmanyan Chandrasekhar used math to explain what can happen to stars much larger than the sun when they run out of energy. When a dying star is at least 20 times the mass of the sun, its own overwhelming gravity crushes the core. In this way, the mass of a dead star can turn into a black hole—a name scientists began using in the 1960s.

Subrahmanyan Chandrasekhar helped explain how a supermassive object can be compressed into a black hole.

Equations and calculations helped scientists learn basic information about black holes. But no equation or calculation could explain what happens deep inside the event horizon. Scientists believe that a black hole's mass is compressed into a tiny point at its core. This point is far smaller than the tip of a pin—so small it cannot be measured. Scientists describe it as one-dimensional, or having no volume at all. They call it a singularity, the source of a black hole's extreme gravity.

WHAT WOULD EINSTEIN SEE?

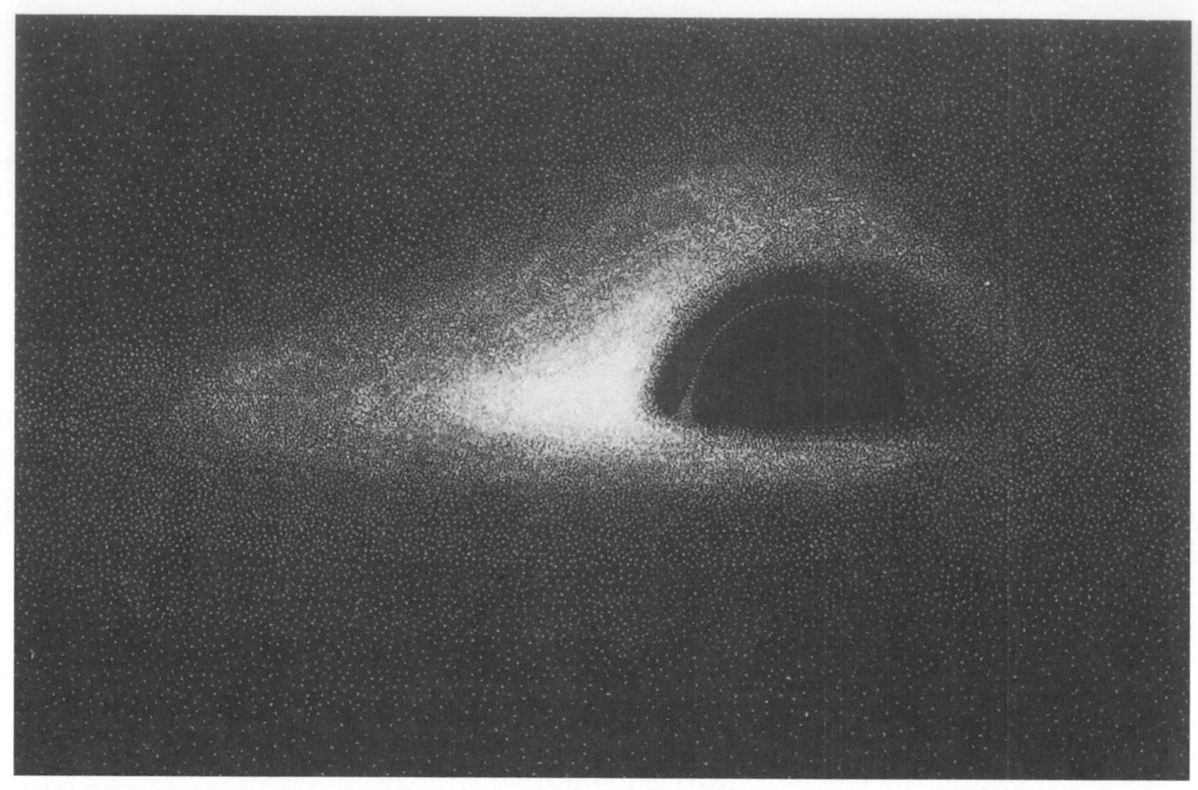

Four decades before a photo of a black hole was taken, Jean-Pierre Luminet used beginning computer imaging along with pen and ink to create a remarkably accurate image of what a black hole might look like.

A French astrophysicist in the late 1970s took up the challenge "to show something of an object that is by definition invisible." Jean-Pierre Luminet used a computer, pen, ink, and photographic paper to create a shadowy image of a black hole. Though computer imaging was basic at that time, the result was startling. A ring framed a black area inside "like a gleaming halo." He used no telescopes of any kind to create it. Instead, he used Einstein's and Schwarzschild's theories and calculations. Their theories stated that extreme gravity bends light like a lens.

Luminet's image revealed a strange landscape. An observer looking at an object with an average gravity, like Saturn, would see the top or underside of its rings. Viewed from the side, part of the rings would disappear, blocked by the planet. But in Luminet's image, the observer sees *both* the top and bottom of the accretion disk—including the part of the disk traveling behind the black hole! With the help of a computer to make calculations, Luminet sketched data as thousands of black dots to create his image. He proudly called his image the "first theoretical glimpse of the shadow of a black hole." The image was published in popular science magazines in 1979. Astronomers admired it and studied it closely.

To escape from inside a black hole's event horizon, a rocket would have to travel faster than the speed of light.

However, scientists were confident about how a black hole looked on the outside—even before ever seeing a photograph of one. Extreme gravity bends space to form a spherical area. So they expected a black hole to look round. They expected this sphere to be black because no light can escape it. Why not? To escape gravity, an object must travel fast enough. A rocket must travel at least 7 miles (11 km) per second to escape Earth's gravity. Because the sun's gravity is stronger, a rocket must travel at least 375 miles (604 km) per second to escape it. To escape from inside a black hole's event horizon, a rocket would have to travel faster than the speed of light.

Scientists also expected a black hole to bend more than space. Extreme gravity also bends time. To an observer, an object approaching a black hole would take a strange journey. It would appear to slow down and then freeze at the edge of the event horizon.

But scientists needed to prove that their theories about black holes were scientific facts. Even Einstein had been reluctant to believe black holes could exist in nature. The hunt for evidence was similar to proving the existence of dinosaurs, Doeleman said. Scientists believe dinosaurs existed even though no one has actually seen one. Their bones and footprints in ancient clay are strong evidence. Even before the 2019 photograph of M87*, scientists had found evidence of black holes too.

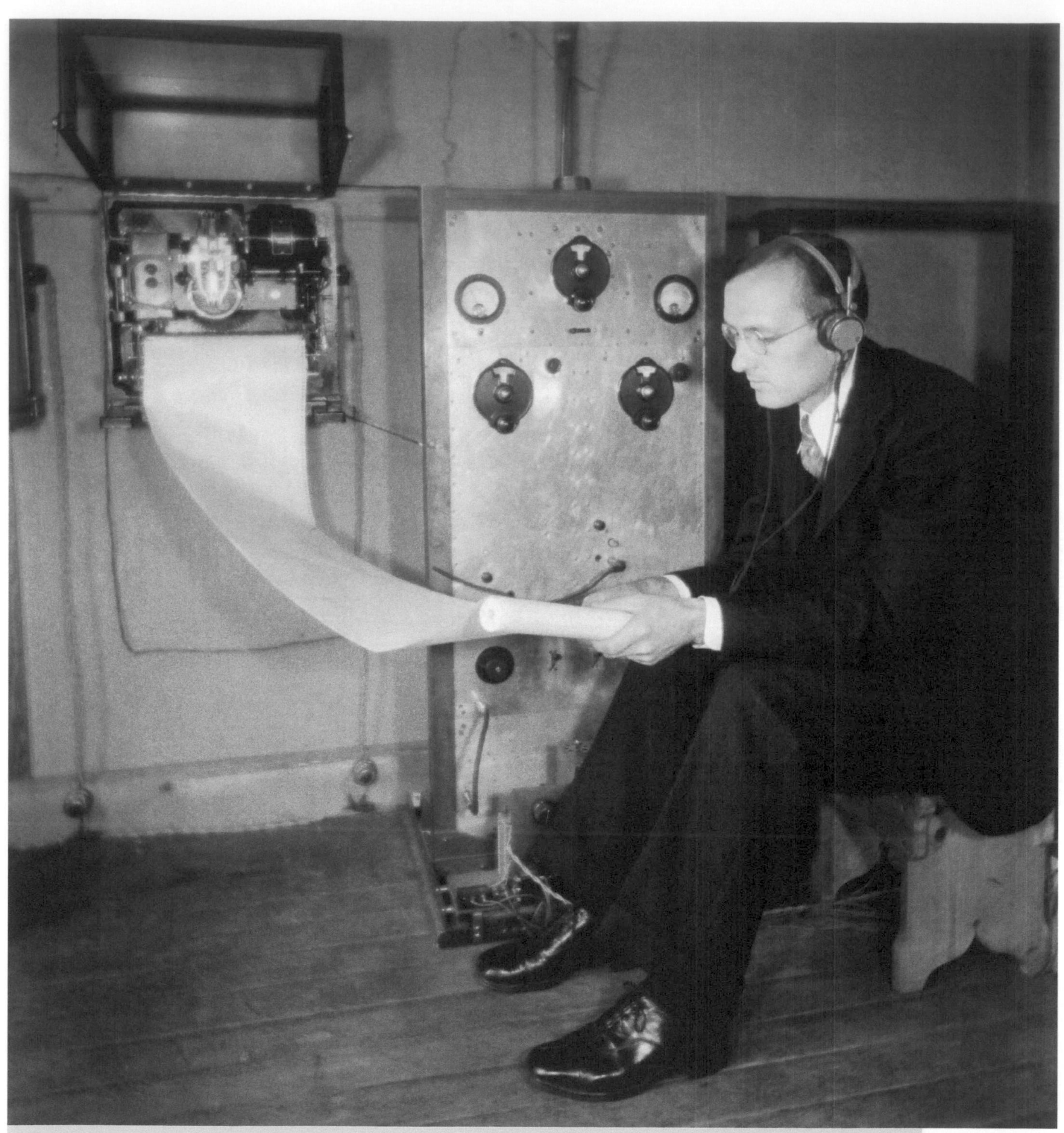

Engineer and physicist Karl Jansky's discovery of radio waves coming from the Milky Way led to the creation of a new area of science called radio astronomy.

A black hole was the source of the first radio signals from space detected on Earth. They were radio waves, recorded in 1932 by engineer and physicist Karl Jansky. He had built a 100-foot (30.5-m) antenna in New Jersey to study radio waves traveling across the Atlantic Ocean. As Jansky was tracking their pattern, he discovered mysterious radio waves coming from somewhere in the center of the Milky Way. Radio astronomers in the 1950s also puzzled over the radio waves bursting from galaxy centers. The energy produced by normal stars to shine could not explain it.

Evidence for black holes and their behavior was beginning to trickle in. Meanwhile, people tried to imagine what they looked like. Artists used their imaginations. Scientists based their drawings on what they knew about how extreme gravity could curve space-time.

Evidence for black holes arrived from space in 1971. Powerful X-rays coming from a star more than 6,000 light-years away in the Milky Way were detected on Earth. Gas and matter from the star traveled around an invisible object. Scientists concluded that only a black hole's gravity could pull the star's matter into such a small orbit. They also concluded that only matter trapped in a black hole's accretion disk could spin quickly enough—and heat up to millions of degrees—to create so many X-rays.

Scientists named the source of the X-rays Cygnus X-1.

A physicist predicted a black hole's shape in 1973. James Bardeen used math to estimate how light would travel near it. He concluded that a black hole passing in front of a bright star would appear as a black circle—like a solar eclipse. He also thought the event horizon would appear to be much larger than it actually is. The extreme gravity warps the path of the light, just as an object seen in water looks magnified. But how could he test this idea? Bardeen was certain it would never be possible to observe this effect.

Astronomers Bruce Balick and Bob Brown located the first black hole—though they were not certain of their discovery at the time. They found the exact location of the source of radio waves bursting from the Milky Way's center in 1974. They used the precision of interferometry—three radio dishes at the Green Bank Observatory in West Virginia and another dish located 22 miles (35 km) away. Balick and Brown named the source of the waves Sagittarius A*. But they did not call their discovery a black hole. There were not enough facts and observations to convince many scientists they existed.

Scientists could not yet photograph black holes, but they could photograph the astonishing effects of their gravity on nearby objects. In the 1990s, scientists used infrared telescopes to photograph stars close to Sagittarius A*. They studied their

In the 1970s, X-ray and optical observations led scientists to the theory that Cygnus X-1 contained a black hole.

positions over several years and noticed something astounding. The stars appeared to orbit an invisible point. And the stars that were the closest to Sagittarius A* whipped around 10 times faster than the stars farther away. Their movements even allowed scientists to predict the mass of the mysterious object they orbited. The size and gravity of this object convinced many that Sagittarius A* could only be a black hole.

Telescopes launched into space have captured dramatic activity around suspected black holes. The Hubble Space Telescope photographed jets, thousands of light-years long, shooting from the center of M87 in 1992. Scientists believe they are evidence of black holes messily swallowing matter. Though some matter falls in, magnetic fields can shoot some of it away at almost the speed of light. In 2004, NASA's Swift telescope captured possible evidence of black holes in bursts of intense light called gamma rays. Scientists concluded the source was stars exploding and collapsing—one way in which scientists believe black holes are formed.

In 2015—a century after Einstein published his theory of gravity—scientists detected powerful waves from space with equipment on Earth. The two detectors of the Laser Interferometer Gravitational-Wave Observatory (LIGO) are spaced more than 2,000 miles (3,220 km) apart in Louisiana and

Washington. They record gravitational waves, or ripples created by gravity. Objects on Earth also create them, but they are too weak to detect. Scientists concluded that LIGO had recorded strong evidence of the collision of two black holes. "But detecting gravitational waves is sort of like hearing

In 1992, the Hubble Telescope photographed jets of plasma thousands of light-years long. Scientists believed that showed that black holes swallow matter while shooting away some of it.

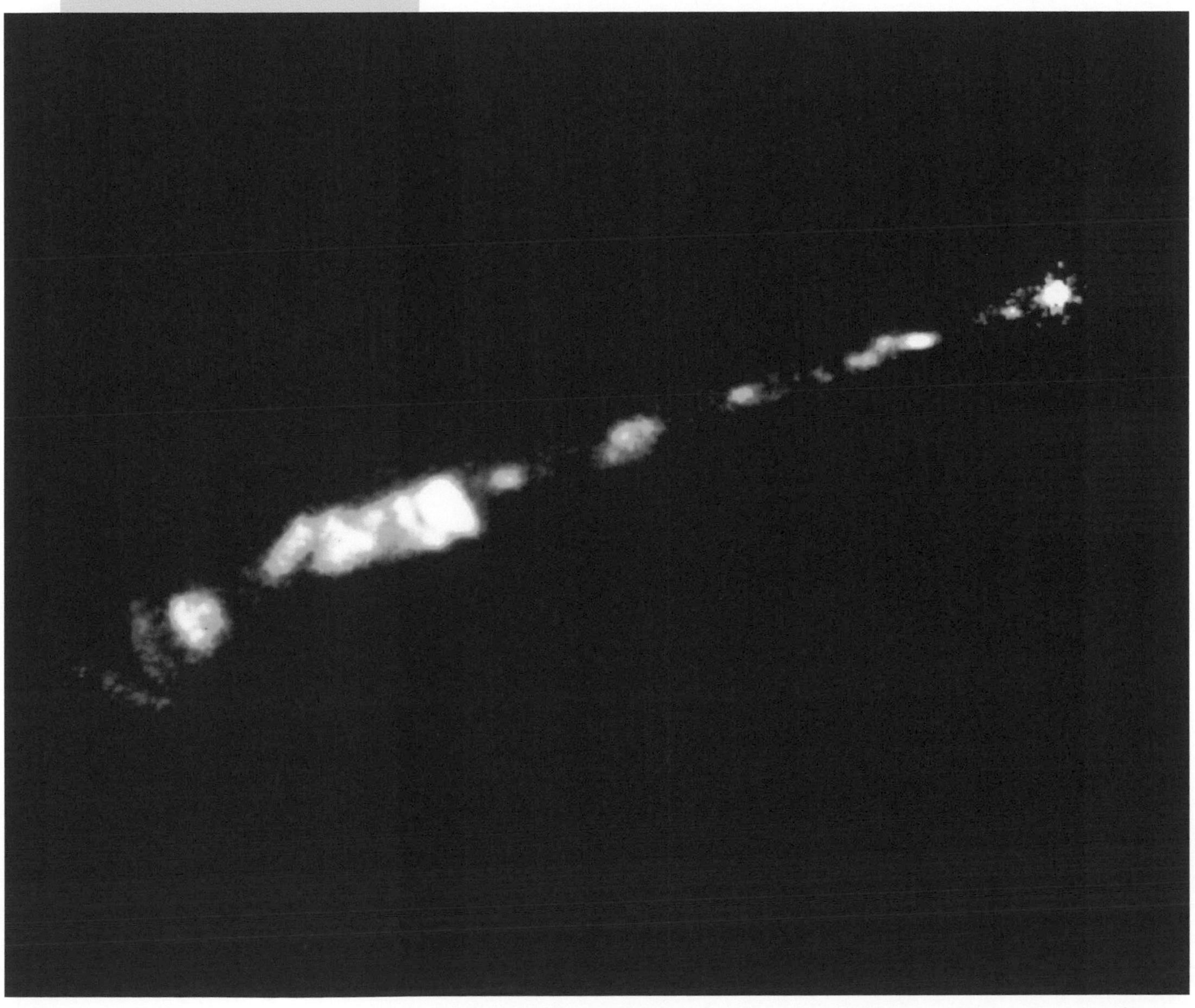

Computer simulation shows how two black holes collided, creating powerful gravitational waves that allowed observers to "hear" this event.

a black hole," explained science writer Davide Castelvecchi. "Scientists still wanted to see it."

Bardeen never made an image based on his ideas. But a group of scientists in the mid-1990s wanted to test his prediction. They used his equations to imagine what Sagittarius A* would look like to a group of telescopes in an Earth-sized VLBI array.

"But detecting gravitational waves is sort of like hearing a black hole," explained science writer Davide Castelvecchi. "Scientists still wanted to see it."

Physicist Eric Agol designed computer software to predict how extreme gravity, like a lens, would bend light. The three scientists decided that Sagittarius A* would look like a dark circle ringed in light. They also concluded that the size of the shadow would depend on the mass of the black hole. Agol, astronomer Heino Falcke, and astrophysicist Fulvio Melia published the results of their work together in 1999. Its title was "Viewing the Shadow of the Black Hole at the Galactic Center." But it was still two decades before scientists put this plan into action with the Event Horizon Telescope (EHT).

For decades, scientists trusted their detailed computer-generated images of black holes. But they also knew that taking a photograph of a black hole is a completely different job. Falcke had proposed the idea of an Earth-sized telescope and collaborated on the EHT. But he expected a disappointing image resembling "an ugly peanut" at best. He was not the only one. "We can run very high-resolution simulations that show a great level of detail, but I'm expecting more of a 'fuzzy blob,'" said Misty Bentz, an astrophysicist at Georgia State University. "It's important to remember that we're talking about pictures of objects that are on the scale of our solar system, but we are viewing them from . . . 54 million light-years away."

ChapterThree

A TWO-YEAR SNAPSHOT

A black hole like M87* is enormous. But it is so far away, it appears impossibly tiny from Earth. Trying to see M87* is as difficult as trying to read the date on a coin in Los Angeles while standing in New York.

Telescopes have come a long way since the 1600s. Views of the moon's craters and Saturn's rings astonished early astronomers. By the 1800s, telescopes could glimpse objects light-years away. Telescopes launched into Earth's orbit gave astronomers the clearest views of our solar system and millions of light-years beyond. But to view M87*, scientists needed a telescope with about 2,000 times the magnifying power of the Hubble Space Telescope. Despite its massive size, M87* appears so small from Earth that it would take about 23 quadrillion black holes like it to fill the visible sky.

Besides distance, there were other challenges that made M87* hard to see. Light waves face many obstacles on their journey from a black hole to a radio telescope. Space is littered with gas, dust, and other debris. It scatters visible light waves and longer radio waves. But short, 1-millimeter-long radio waves make it through. Turbulence also ripples through regions of space like air currents that disturb a cruising airplane. Since the 1990s, astronomers tried

The launch of the Hubble Space Telescope in 1990 was a major achievement, but its magnifying power wasn't nearly enough to capture an image of a black hole.

to glimpse the suspected black hole, Sagittarius A*, through this churning fog. "It's like looking through frosted glass," explained Doeleman.

The public was eager to finally see a black hole. Newspapers and news websites had published the exciting study in 2000 that proposed it was possible. For nearly two decades, Doeleman spoke to people who could donate funds or telescopes to the EHT. He needed to convince them that trying to photograph a black hole was worth the time and money. His passion for the project attracted other black hole hunters. Astronomers, astrophysicists, researchers, engineers, and computer programmers began joining his team in the early 2000s. They jumped into the VLBI experiments.

Doeleman's team organized its first observation with a VLBI array in 2006. The team linked up observatories in Arizona and Hawaii to observe Sagittarius A*. Its attempt was a disaster. Because of a broken part inside a circuit board, no useful data were recorded.

The telescope in Hawaii was one of two linked to try to look at a black hole in 2006. It failed miserably because of a technical problem.

"You have to be optimistic and confident that you are on the right path."

But Doeleman did not give up. "You have to be optimistic and confident that you are on the right path," he said.

The following year the team tried again. A California observatory joined the telescope array. This time the team detected something at the heart of the Milky Way. There was not enough data to make an image—but what team members saw was the size of the event horizon of Sagittarius A*, confirming their predictions.

In 2009, Doeleman's team made one more stunning discovery: M87*—a black hole in the distant Virgo constellation. It is about 2,000 times as far away as Sagittarius A*. But M87* is enormous compared to Sagittarius A*. Its mass is about 1,000 times greater. Doeleman's array detected its shadow even at its great distance.

In 2012, Doeleman's team officially named its project the Event Horizon Telescope. It was the year the array peered through the veils of space debris. Though the array could not see M87*, it got close. The 12-hour observation by the three telescopes captured the rotating movement and direction of M87*'s accretion disk. It also revealed the size of its inner edge, which was about five solar systems wide. That means the black hole—at billions of times the sun's mass—really does pack immense mass into a tiny area.

To photograph the black hole's shadow, scientists needed the most advanced electronics available to date. The EHT team purchased equipment. Team members designed some of it themselves, such as the tools that converted information from radio waves into digital code. New data recorders could capture data arriving at the rate of about 64 gigabits per second. That's about 1,000 times faster than a home internet connection. To keep so much data organized, atomic clocks the size of small refrigerators added time stamps. EHT team members traveled in planes and up mountain roads in trucks to observatories. They installed the equipment to enable observatories to join a global VLBI array.

But the EHT also needed more telescopes. Doeleman wanted eight, and one in particular. Many astronomers waited for a chance to use Chile's Atacama Large Millimeter Array (ALMA). Its array of 66 dishes functions like a single dish 46,000 feet (14,000 m) wide. That's powerful enough to focus on a golf ball 9 miles (14.5 km) away. The EHT team delayed its observation until 2017 in order to reserve time on ALMA. It boosted the power of the EHT tenfold. It could now see objects one-ten-thousandth the size of what the Hubble Space Telescope can see.

"ALMA changed everything," said EHT astronomer Vincent Fish. "Anything that you were

New data recorders could capture data arriving at the rate of about 64 gigabits per second. That's about 1,000 times faster than a home internet connection.

Chile's Atacama Large Millimeter Array was crucial to the success of the EHT's attempt to obtain the first image of a black hole.

just barely struggling to detect before, you get really solid detections now."

Thanks to ALMA and the rest of the EHT, the 2017 observation gathered an enormous amount of data. But its journey to becoming a photograph was long and complex. First, EHT teams near Boston and in Bonn, Germany, used supercomputers to smooth out problems during the observations of both black holes—wobbles in Earth's movements and small lapses in the atomic clocks. These machines also combined all the data by matching up the time

Scientists have long hypothesized what a black hole might look like. This computer-generated image shows a black hole surrounded by swirling matter that forms a glowing accretion disc.

stamps. The first results revealed that M87*'s data were clearer than Sagittarius A*'s.

Putting together a photograph of M87* could fail, even with excellent data. Mirrored tiles cover a radio telescope's dish completely. But the EHT functions like an Earth-sized dish covered only with a few mirrored tiles—at the eight locations of the observatories in the array. "This is an incredibly small number of measurements to make a picture from . . . there are an infinite number of possible images that are perfectly consistent with our telescope measurements," explained Katie Bouman.

A photograph of a black hole would be a powerful test of all black hole theories.

The EHT project would fail if scientists relied on hypotheses. To see how a black hole really looked, they had to ignore ideas of how a black hole should look. Doeleman expected to see a "ring of light around the black hole. And the size and shape of that was predicted by Einstein." A photograph of a black hole would be a powerful test of all black hole theories.

How could the EHT team feel confident about a photograph of an object no one had ever seen? Bouman explained the challenge. The EHT team had to use telescope data the way a police sketch artist uses eyewitnesses' details to draw a portrait of a suspect. The team had to fill in gaps between bits of data. But team members could not shape the data to fit their hypotheses of the mystery object's appearance.

The EHT team set up a way to keep themselves open-minded. In mid-2018, EHT scientists broke into four groups to create unique images based on the same EHT data. They gave computers complex instructions, called algorithms, for assembling bits of information. Einstein's predictions, or any of the scientists' expectations, played no direct part in these instructions. Two groups relied on an algorithm used by radio astronomers since the 1970s. The other two groups used a brand-new algorithm designed in 2016 by Bouman and her team. Each group worked independently and in secrecy.

A HANDS-ON SCIENTIST

Shep Doeleman happily spoke at a press conference after announcing the success of the EHT project in 2019.

Radio telescope images of light exploding from galaxies inspired young Shep Doeleman to wonder about black holes. *Whatever is powering those jets has to be insanely powerful,* he remembered thinking. He studied astrophysics and learned to work the hard math of Einstein's theories. But he was happiest working in observatories from Antarctica to Massachusetts. His job as EHT director sent him to observatories around the world, to remote and high locations. There he built a deep knowledge of the complex wires, mirrors, and machinery of radio telescopes.

Doeleman had to develop new skills to lead the EHT team. He had to learn how to manage people involved in the $50 million project. The EHT team had just 25 members in 2008 but had grown to hundreds by 2019. The stress was so great he once said he felt like coal crushed into a diamond by the pressure. But he never forgot the reason that kept him and his team enthusiastic. "We set our sights high, and we took on the biggest questions that we could think of to ask: What is the nature of a black hole? How does it work?" Doeleman said later. "And then we said, 'Can we image it to answer these questions?' And we just didn't take no for an answer."

“This is the moment when we finally get to see what a black hole might look like.”

Members of each group gathered in a Cambridge, Massachusetts, office on June 25, 2018. It was the same room that had served as the command center during the 2017 EHT observation. Doeleman watched as the four scientists prepared to feed new EHT data into the algorithms loaded on their laptops. “This is the moment when we finally get to see what a black hole might look like,” Doeleman said. So much could change in this moment. If the object was not round or if it was smaller than expected, it might not be a black hole. A weird and unexpected image could even prove Einstein’s equations wrong.

“Let’s see it,” he told the team.

Bouman counted down and said, “OK, ready . . . set . . . go.” All four scientists pressed a laptop key and the algorithms went to work. Everyone watched shapes appear on the monitors. “What I’m seeing on the screen is pretty startling,” Doeleman said. “If this holds up, it’s going to be the discovery of my lifetime, and I think of many other people’s lifetimes.”

Each of the four images showed a glowing ring of about the same size. And each framed a dark area: the black hole’s shadow. They were not identical, yet they were so similar. “It was a remarkable moment,” said astrophysicist Kazunori Akiyama, who helped lead one of the four groups.

For Doeleman, the combined images were the result of years of building the EHT and its team. "So we see this ring. It's phenomenal," he later remembered. He admitted feeling great relief. "You know what I was really expecting to see? A blob."

To the trained eyes of scientists, the image was no blob. They were stunned and excited by what they saw. The photograph proved that decades of research on a distant and unseen object had been accurate. "It's almost scarily as we predicted," said EHT astrophysicist Sera Markoff.

The bright ring in the photograph was lopsided, as expected. Light from the rotating accretion ring behaves like sound from a passing police car. As the siren draws closer, the sound grows higher. Then it drops as it moves away. Light from the rotating accretion disk looks brighter as it approaches. It looks dimmer when it moves away. This observation also told scientists that this black hole spins in a clockwise direction.

Scientists could finally measure a black hole with confidence. M87*'s event horizon is almost the size of the entire solar system. It measures about 24 billion miles (38.6 billion km) across.

With this measurement, the team calculated its mass at 6.5 billion times the sun's mass—that's about the mass calculated by observing the movement of stars and gas.

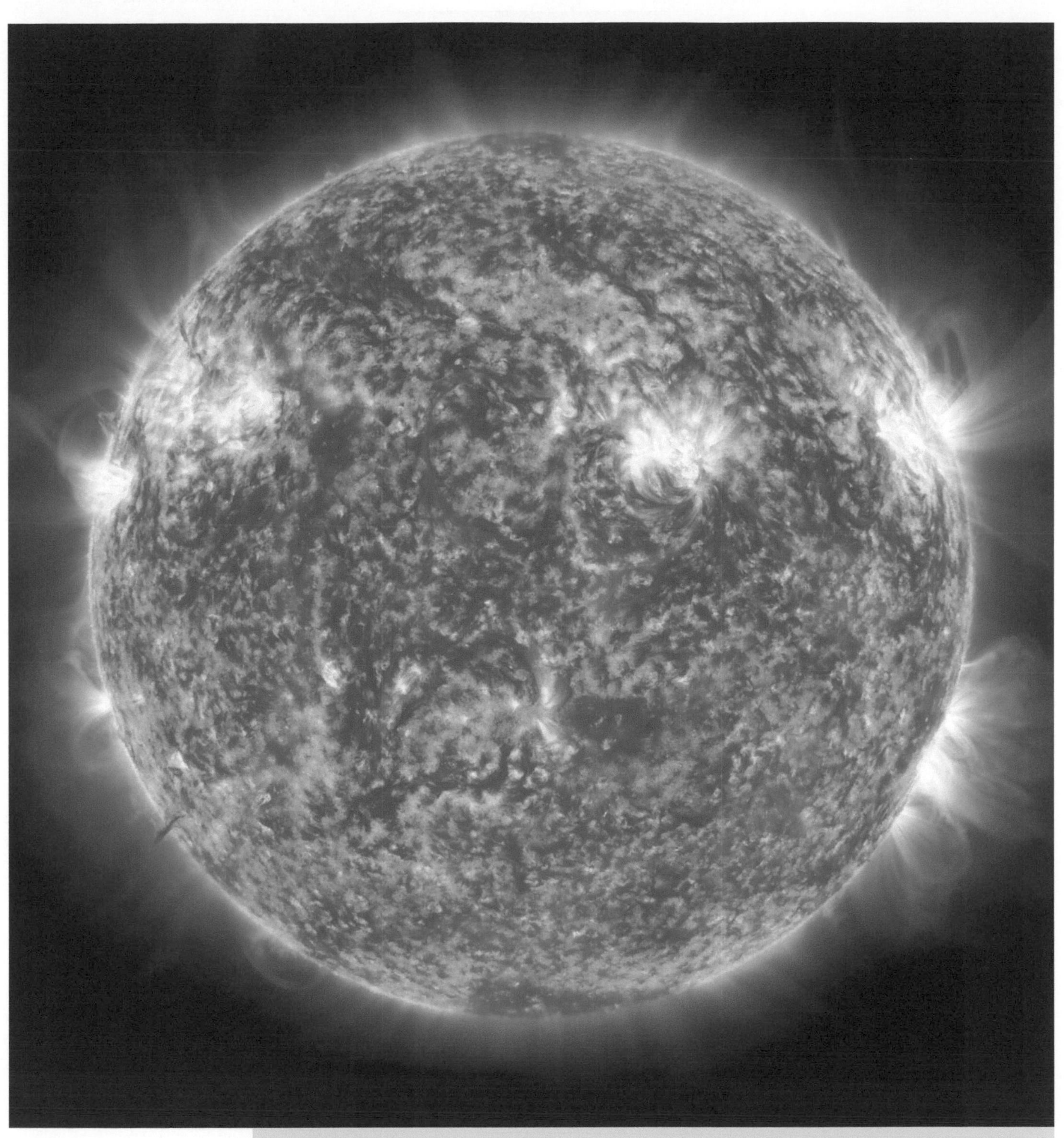

How big is a black hole? Our sun—shown here—is equal to the mass of 332,946 Earths. The mass of the black hole Doeleman's team imaged is 6.5 billion times that of the sun!

The four images produced from EHT data and algorithms were combined into a single image. This is the image the world would see a year later. Why didn't Doeleman and his team rush to share at least a hint of this exciting news? Because scientists test everything for accuracy before publishing their findings.

Team members ran thousands of simulations of how M87* might look with small changes. For example, what if the accretion disk were a different temperature? What if it spun differently? The simulations brought good news. It turns out that the photograph is difficult to tell apart from the simulations. The photograph had passed the test. It was a reasonable image of a black hole based on the EHT data.

For EHT scientists, the final photograph was captivating. Looking at the photograph "was surprisingly emotional . . . we've been looking at pictures quite similar to that from our own models," remembered Markoff. "But when you look at it and you have to tell yourself that it's actually data, that you're not seeing a simulation but you're really looking at a black hole, I found myself just with my cell phone staring at it for hours."

It's likely that most of the 350 people from 20 countries who worked on the EHT project felt the same way. For Doeleman, the photograph

The photograph had passed the test. It was a reasonable image of a black hole based on the EHT data.

is about “the human story of colleagues working together, across borders, to turn our planet into an immense lens. It makes you feel that nothing is impossible.”

ChapterFour
SEEING IS BELIEVING

EHT team members presented their photograph to the world at simultaneous press conferences on April 10, 2019. Its glowing ring projected on screens above the presenters in the U.S., Belgium, Denmark, Chile, China, Japan, and Taiwan. “We have seen and taken a picture of a black hole,” announced Doeleman in Washington, D.C. The glowing ring soon appeared on TV newscasts, newspaper front pages, and in social media.

The popularity of the photograph amazed Doeleman. It reminded him of the impact of another famous image: the 1968 photograph of the blue sphere of Earth taken by Apollo 8 astronauts orbiting the moon. “It really put things in perspective for us, it made us feel connected in a way that we hadn’t before, it made us feel vulnerable,” Doeleman explained. “These are iconic images; they’re terrifying, but we can’t look away.”

For many scientists, the image brought great relief. Einstein’s theories proved true once again. M87* warped space-time as predicted by Einstein’s math. Even a glance at the photograph proved it. Einstein and Schwarzschild had predicted a black hole would be circular. Its size fits Schwarzschild’s calculations too. Scientists have accepted Einstein’s

Shep Doeleman and team members showed the first photo of the black hole at a press conference in Washington, D.C., on April 10, 2019.

theories for more than a century. The EHT provided direct evidence for them. "There is nothing better than having an image," said astrophysicist Avi Loeb. "Seeing is believing."

A few scientists felt disappointed that the photograph so closely matched expectations. EHT astrophysicist Avery Broderick had made models to predict what the EHT would find. "I have to admit that I was a little stunned that it matched so closely the predictions that we had made. It's gratifying, sometimes frustrating." Astrophysics professor Jenny

The image of the black hole rocked the world as nothing had since the photo of Earth taken by Apollo 8 astronauts that came to be known as the "blue marble."

Greene wished the photograph was more surprising. "Did the modeling have to work so well? After all that work, couldn't we just get a hint of new physics?"

But the EHT's first, fuzzy photograph may help explain other important questions. Scientists can

"Did the modeling have to work so well? After all that work, couldn't we just get a hint of new physics?"

study the image for clues about magnetic fields. It could explain how jets shoot from the center of supermassive black holes like M87*. These black holes are too massive to have formed from a dead star. Scientists believe they formed billions of years ago when the universe was young. The eating and belching habits of supermassive black holes could help explain how matter in the universe is recycled and reshaped by these powerful jets.

The EHT photograph could help change old ideas about black holes. Once they were seen only as the bathtub drains of the universe, a one-way entrance for matter and light. But during the 2017 observation, EHT data revealed changes in the black hole's changing appearance over just a few days. This data proved that black holes are complex and energetic, as physicist Stephen Hawking predicted beginning in the late 1970s. As a world-famous black hole expert, Hawking proposed many ideas. Black holes may evaporate. They may record information about all the matter that disappears into the event horizon. And the event horizon may even emit faint light.

The EHT photograph inspired a nickname for M87*. It captured the power and energy of the black hole: Powehi. In the Hawaiian language that means "dark source of creation." Larry Kimura, a professor at the University of Hawaii, chose it. Two telescopes in the EHT are located in that state.

The EHT photograph revealed that black holes are far from static. In this artist's rendering, turbulent winds of gas swirl around a black hole. Some of the gas spirals toward the hole while another part is blown away.

Sagittarius A* data from the 2017 observation awaited. The team had avoided tackling its data first because it was less clear. Its size is one reason. Since it is far smaller than M87*, matter and light orbit around it more frequently. That means that the EHT recorded more changes in its appearance than in M87*'s. Turning this data into a photo will require more advanced computer technology and algorithms. But the reward may be worth the extra effort. Sagittarius A* data may provide more detailed information about black holes than M87*. Scientists also hope that a photograph of Sagittarius A* will allow them to compare an inactive black hole with an active black hole.

Collecting new and better data with the EHT was the team's goal, even in busy 2019. In April of that year—the same month the first photograph captured the world's attention—team members turned the EHT on once again. This time the array included a telescope in Greenland. The observation of the Milky Way and M87* lasted a week. The team recorded twice as much data as it had in 2017. With the new data, scientists could confirm what they already knew about black holes. They might also discover something new. But the wild success of their 2019 image did not mean they would rush. "The plan is to carry out these observations indefinitely and see how things change," Doeleman explained. By then, the EHT will include two more telescopes in its array. One is in the French Alps. The other is in a country in southern Africa called Namibia. "They'll fill out that virtual mirror that we're trying to build," Doeleman said.

How do you expand an Earth-sized VLBI array? Telescopes must be placed beyond the planet's surface. "World domination is not enough for us; we also want to go into space," Falcke said. He imagined launching a radio telescope in Earth's orbit. It could record clearer data as it sails high above weather or Earth's wobbles.

The NOrthern Extended Millimeter Array (NOEMA) in the French Alps is one of the world's most advanced facilities for radio astronomy. Once all 12 antennas are installed, it will be the most powerful such telescope in the northern hemisphere.

Some estimate that an array of radio telescopes in space could view targets five times more clearly than the Earth-sized EHT.

What if a VLBI array could show viewers on Earth matter falling into a black hole or spewing out in jets? What if radio telescopes allowed viewers to spy a black hole that closely? "We want to make a movie in real time of things orbiting around the black hole," Doeleman said. "That's what we want to do over the next decade." He estimates that with an array of 20 telescopes, it could one day be possible.

WOMEN ON THE TEAM

Katie Bouman was an integral member of the team that took the first photograph of a black hole.

A photograph of EHT computer scientist Katie Bouman went viral on April 10, 2019. The 29-year-old PhD student was captured in front of her laptop. Its screen displayed the image her algorithm produced of M87*. Many people shared the image of the young scientist smiling at the result of her and her team's creativity and hard work. The team had worked for six years to develop the algorithm that helped make the photograph possible.

Bouman wanted to encourage other young people to find the same joy. "If you study things like computer science and electrical engineering, it's not just building circuits in your lab," Bouman said. "You can go out to a telescope at 15,000 feet above sea level, and you can use those skills to do something that no one's ever done before."

Bouman is one of about 40 female EHT team members. She and others hope to inspire girls to pursue their dreams of studying science. "There are women involved in every single step of this amazing project," said Dutch graduate student and EHT team member Sara Issaoun. "As a woman in STEM myself, it's good to have role models out there who young girls and young boys can look up to."

This NASA telescope image shows the Messier 87 galaxy, the home galaxy of the black hole photographed by Doeleman's team. The top inset shows a closeup of two shockwaves created by a jet coming from the black hole. The second inset shows a closeup image of the black hole's silhouette.

What a black hole hunter wants to see most of all is its greatest mystery: the inside of it. But "the universe has cloaked it in the ultimate invisibility cloak," said Doeleman. "So, we don't know what happens in there." Scientists continue to develop and revise ideas about what could happen inside a black hole. They predict what would happen to a visitor falling into an event horizon. In a supermassive black hole like M87*, a person would feel weightless and fall peacefully toward the center of the black hole—until reaching the singularity. In smaller black holes, gravity would pull strongly on the body as the extreme gravity increased. The body would stretch as thin as a noodle, and finally into a string of atoms. Scientists struggle to make hypotheses about what happens to matter there. "We don't have the physics to explain what a black hole is," said astronomer Andrea Ghez. It "leads to a paradox, a breakdown in our understanding of how the universe works."

Some scientists wrestle with theories. Others, such as Doeleman, work to bring the universe's mysteries close with their images. "We've seen the shadow of a black hole, but this story is just beginning," Doeleman said. "We've opened a window onto the event horizon that we never had before. We don't know how this book is going to end. All we know is that the first chapter has us hooked, and that's enough."

Timeline

1783

Scientist John Mitchell proposes the theory that "dark stars" exist and trap light with their extreme gravity.

1915

Physicist Albert Einstein publishes his general theory of relativity, which describes how mass curves space and time, which he calls "space-time."

1916

Astronomer Karl Schwarzschild solves Einstein's equations to calculate how an object could trap light.

1964

A reporter covering a meeting of scientists in Cleveland coins the term *black hole* in an article in *Science News Letter*. Later in the decade, physicist John Wheeler popularizes the term.

1971

Scientists name a source of X-rays Cygnus X-1. Some scientists believe that only a black hole could heat up its matter to such an intense degree.

1930s

Astrophysicist Subrahmanyan Chandrasekhar uses math to explain how stars can collapse into objects of extreme gravity.

1932

Physicist Karl Jansky detects the first radio waves from space with a 100-foot (30-meter) antenna.

1973

Physicist James Bardeen calculates how a star's light would be distorted when passing near a black hole.

1974

Astronomers Bruce Balick and Bob Brown use VLBI to identify radio waves emitted by a suspected black hole at the center of the Milky Way. They name it Sagittarius A*.

Timeline

1974

Physicist Stephen Hawking upends black hole theory. He proposes that a black hole may evaporate and emit dim light from its event horizon.

1978

Scientists tracking star movements at the center of M87 suspect it contains a supermassive black hole.

1990s

Astronomers observe star movement to predict the mass of suspected black holes.

2008

Early members of the Event Horizon Telescope discover evidence of a suspected black hole at the center of the Milky Way with a three-telescope VLBI array.

2012

Shep Doeleman and his team formally launch the EHT project at a meeting at the University of Arizona.

2015

LIGO detects powerful gravitational waves from space. Scientists determine their source is two black holes colliding and merging.

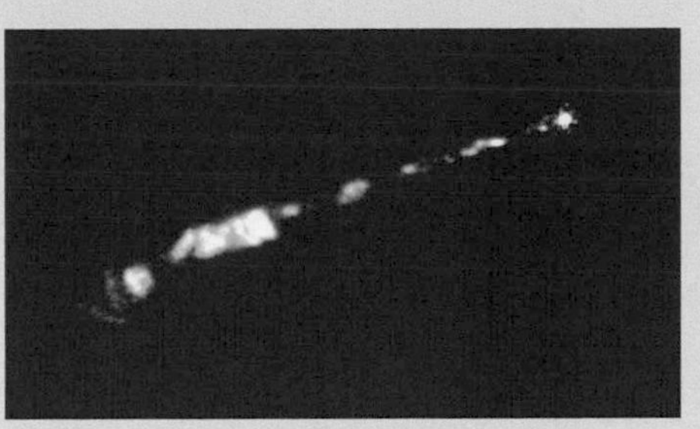

1992

The Hubble Space Telescope captures clear images of jets shooting from the suspected black hole at the center of M87.

1999

Astronomer Heino Falcke, physicist Eric Agol, and astrophysicist Fulvio Melia publish a scientific paper about how a black hole would appear to an Earth-sized telescope, as predicted by computer software.

2017

The EHT team conducts an observation in April using a VLBI array of telescopes in eight locations.

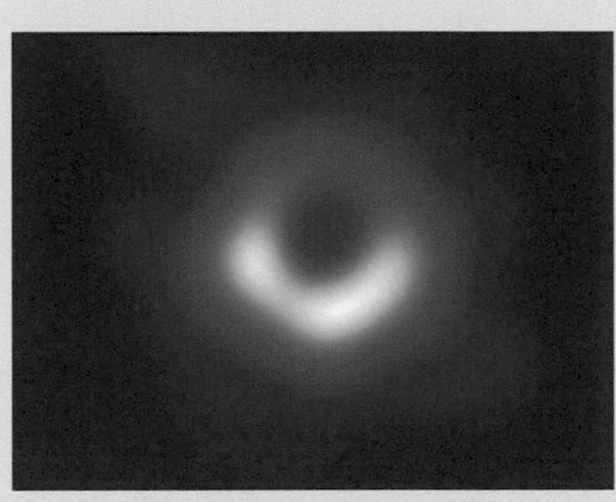

2019

The EHT team presents the first photograph of a black hole.

Glossary

accretion—the process of growing by slowly adding layers of matter

algorithm—a set of rules that guide calculations and problem-solving, usually by a computer

array—an orderly series or arrangement

atomic clock—the most precise mechanism for measuring time, based on the movement of atoms; it loses accuracy by only a second about every 30 billion years

baseline—the distance between two radio telescopes in an array

data—information that can be used in calculating, reasoning, or planning

dense—marked by compactness or crowding together of parts

event horizon—the boundary around a black hole where gravity is so strong that light cannot escape it

gravity—the force that attracts two objects with mass to each other

hypothesis—an idea or explanation based on information already known or observed, which can be tested with experiments

interferometry—a technique in which waves—usually electromagnetic or sound—are compared to each other to discover the patterns that provide information about a distant source

light-year—the distance light travels in a year, which equals almost 6 trillion miles (about 9.5 trillion kilometers)

magnetic field—an area where particles, such as electrons, are charged with energy and exert magnetic force

mass—a measurement of how much matter an object contains, calculated by how an object responds to being set in motion

observatory—a building that houses telescopes and equipment for studying objects and events in space and on Earth, such as weather

petabyte—1 million gigabytes (one gigabyte equals 1 billion bytes)

radius—a straight line extending from the center of a circle to the outside edge or from the center of a sphere to the surface

simulation—the process of creating a model of a real-life object or situation

singularity—an infinitely small, one-dimensional point that contains enormous mass

space-time—the idea that three-dimensional space and time are fused in a four-dimensional system

theory—an explanation for why or how things happen, based on scientific observations and experiments

Additional Resources

Further Reading

DeCristofano, Carolyn Cinami. *A Black Hole Is Not a Hole*. Watertown, MA: Charlesbridge Publishing, 2017.

DK Publishing. *The Astronomy Book: Big Ideas Simply Explained*. London: DK Publishing, 2017.

Oseid, Kelsey. *What We See in the Stars: An Illustrated Tour of the Night Sky*. New York: Ten Speed Press, 2017.

Tyson, Neil deGrasse. *Astrophysics for Young People in a Hurry*. New York: Norton Young Readers, 2019.

Internet Sites

ALMA Website for Kids
http://kids.alma.cl/?lang=en#

NASA Science Space Place
https://spaceplace.nasa.gov/black-holes/en/

What Do Radio Waves Tell Us about the Universe?
https://kids.frontiersin.org/article/10.3389/frym.2016.00002

Critical Thinking Questions

A black hole "leads to a paradox, a breakdown in our understanding of how the universe works," said astronomer Andrea Ghez. A paradox is like a puzzle that seems to have no logical solution. What characteristics of a black hole make it a paradox?

How did nature make a black hole difficult to photograph? What factors made it possible for the EHT to finally photograph it? Consider factors on Earth, in space, and around and inside a black hole itself.

The EHT team depended on the latest technology to photograph a black hole. But how did the project depend as much on people? Find examples of how the project could have failed without the team members' logic, creativity, and spirit.

Source Notes

p. 9, "Imagine taking a hammer..." Deborah Netburn, "Here it is, the first-ever image of a black hole." *Los Angeles Times*, April 10, 2019, https://www.latimes.com/science/sciencenow/la-sci-sn-black-hole-first-picture-event-horizon-201904010-story.html Accessed October 23, 2019.

p. 10, "I think we should call it a go..." Seth Fletcher. *Einstein's Shadow: A Black Hole, a Band of Astronomers, and the Quest to See the Unseeable*. New York: Ecco, 2018, p. 209.

p. 10, "Five. Four. Three. Two..." Ibid., p. 210.

p. 12, "an astonishing spate of planet-wide good weather..." Dave Mosher, "Like looking at the gates of Hell: Astronomers just revealed the first picture of a black hole, and it's a monster," *Business Insider*, April 10, 2019, https://www.businessinsider.com/supermassive-black-hole-first-photo-event-horizon-telescope-m87-2019-4 Accessed October 23, 2019.

p. 12, "You really feel..." "Portrait of a Shadow, The Event Horizon Telescope," *Black Hole Initiative*, 4:43, https://bhi.fas.harvard.edu/ Accessed October 23, 2019.

p. 13, "we basically had to freeze light..." Abigail Hess, "29-year-old Katie Bouman 'didn't know anything about black holes'—then she helped capture the first photo of one," CNBC, April 12, 2019, https://www.cnbc.com/2019/04/12/katie-bouman-helped-generate-the-first-ever-photo-of-a-black-hole.html Accessed October 23, 2019.

p. 13, "the entire selfie collection..." Nadia Drake, "First-ever picture of a black hole unveiled," *National Geographic*, April 10, 2019, https://www.nationalgeographic.com/science/2019/04/first-picture-black-hole-revealed-m87-event-horizon-telescope-astrophysics/ Accessed October 13, 2019.

p. 15, "We have seen what we thought was unseeable..." Dennis Overbye, "Darkness Visible, Finally: Astronomers Capture First Ever Image of a Black Hole," *New York Times*, April 10, 2019, https://www.nytimes.com/2019/04/10/science/black-hole-picture.html Accessed October 13, 2019.

p. 16, "We've been studying black holes..." Marina Koren, "An Extraordinary Image of the Black Hole at a Galaxy's Heart." *Atlantic*, April 10, 2019, https://www.theatlantic.com/science/archive/2019/04/black-hole-event-horizon-telescope/586846/ Accessed October 13, 2019.

p. 18, "If you took a baseball..." "Here It Is, The First-ever Image of a Black Hole."

p. 20, "to show something of an object..." Daniel Clery, "Here's what scientists think a black hole looks like." *Science*, April 8, 2019, https://www.sciencemag.org/news/2019/04/here-s-what-scientists-think-black-hole-looks Accessed October 23, 2019.

p. 20, "like a gleaming halo..." Jean-Pierre Luminet, "An Illustrated History of Black Hole Imaging: Personal Recollections (1972-2002)," Cornell University, https://arxiv.org/pdf/1902.11196.pdf Accessed October 13, 2019.

p. 20, "first theoretical glimpse..." Ibid.

p. 27, "But detecting gravitational waves..." Davide Castelvecchi, "Black hole pictured for first time—in spectacular detail," *Nature*, April 10, 2019, https://www.nature.com/articles/d41586-019-01155-0 1:05, Accessed October 13, 2019.

p. 29, "We can run..." Dave Mosher, "The first 'groundbreaking' pictures of a black hole may be unveiled on Wednesday. Here's what scientists think those images will look like," *Business Insider*, April 9, 2019, https://www.businessinsider.com/black-hole-event-horizon-telescope-first-pictures-simulated-2019-4 Accessed October 23, 2019.

p. 31, "It's like looking through frosted glass..." Dennis Overbye, "Darkness Visible."

p. 33, "You have to be optimistic and confident that you are on the right path," "Why the Event Horizon Telescope Took So Long to Image a Black Hole."

p. 34, "ALMA changed everything..." Maria Temming, "How scientists took the first picture of a black hole," *Science News*, April 10, 2019, https://www.sciencenews.org/article/event-horizon-telescope-black-hole-picture Accessed October 13, 2019.

p. 36, "This is an incredibly small number..." Katie Bouman, "How to take a picture of a black hole," TedXBeaconStreet, November 2016, https://www.ted.com/talks/katie_bouman_what_does_a_black_hole_look_like/transcript?language=en Accessed October 13, 2019.

p. 37, "ring of light..." Christopher Intagliata, "SciFri Extra: Picturing a Black Hole," Science Friday, April 8, 2019, https://www.sciencefriday.com/articles/picturing-a-black-hole/ Accessed October 13, 2019.

p. 38, "Whatever is powering..." Dennis Overbye, "Black Hole Hunters," *New York Times*, June 8, 2015, https://www.nytimes.com/2015/06/09/science/black-hole-event-horizon-telescope.html Accessed October 23, 2019.

p. 38, "We set our sights high..." Mike Wall, "Event Horizon Telescope Team Wins $3 Million Breakthrough Prize for Epic Black Hole Imagery," *Space*, September 5, 2019, https://www.space.com/event-horizon-telescope-breakthrough-prize.html Accessed October 23, 2019.

p. 39, "This is the moment..." "Black Hole Hunters," Smithsonian Channel, https://www.youtube.com/watch?v=GgfySOiJ6Oc 0:52, Accessed October 13, 2019.

p. 39, "Let's see it..." "Event Horizon Telescope Team Wins $3 Million Breakthrough Prize for Epic Black Hole Imagery."

p. 39, "Ok, ready...set...go..." Ibid.

p. 39, "What I'm seeing on the screen..." Ibid.

p. 39, "It was a remarkable moment," Andrew Grant, "What it took to capture a black hole," *Physics Today*, April 11, 2019, https://physicstoday.scitation.org/do/10.1063/PT.6.1.20190411a/full/ Accessed October 13, 2019.

p. 40, "So we see this ring..." "Portrait of a Shadow, The Event Horizon Telescope," *Black Hole Initiative*, 7:15, https://bhi.fas.harvard.edu/ Accessed October 23, 2019.

p. 40, "You know what I was really expecting to see?" "Black hole pictured for first time—in spectacular detail."

p. 40, "is almost scarily..." Nadia Drake, "First-ever picture of a black hole unveiled," *National Geographic*, April 10, 2019, https://www.nationalgeographic.com/science/2019/04/first-picture-black-hole-revealed-m87-event-horizon-telescope-astrophysics/ Accessed October 13, 2019.

p. 42, "was surprisingly emotional..." "Portrait of a Shadow."

p. 43, "the human story of colleagues working..." Peter Reuell, "Black Hole Project Nets Breakthrough Prize," *Harvard Gazette*, September 5, 2019, https://news.harvard.edu/gazette/story/2019/09/black-hole-project-nets-breakthrough-prize/ Accessed October 23, 2019.

p. 44, "We have seen..." Maria Temming, "How scientists took the first picture of a black hole." *Science News*, April 10, 2019, https://www.sciencenews.org/article/event-horizon-telescope-black-hole-picture Accessed October 13, 2019.

p. 44, "It really put things in perspective..." Meghan Bartels, "The Scientists Behind the First

Source Notes

Black Hole Photo Get Nod from Congress," *Space*, May 17, 2019, https://www.space.com/first-black-hole-photo-science-team-meets-congress.html Accessed October 13, 2019.

p. 45, "There is nothing better…" "How Scientists Took the First Picture of a Black Hole."

p. 45, "I have to admit…" Jenny Greene, "The black hole photo was no big surprise to scientists. Here's why it's still a big deal," *Washington Post*, April 12, 2019, https://www.washingtonpost.com/opinions/2019/04/12/black-hole-photo-was-no-big-surprise-scientists-heres-why-its-still-big-deal/ Accessed October 13, 2019.

p. 46, "Did the modeling have to work *so* well?…" Ibid.

p. 47, "dark souce of creation…" Rafi Letzter, "3 Huge Questions the Black Hole Image Didn't Answer," *LiveScience*, April 10, 2019, https://www.livescience.com/65200-black-hole-event-horizon-image-questions-remain.html Accessed October 13, 2019.

p. 49, "The plan is…" "Darkness Visible."

p. 49, "They'll fill out…" "Event Horizon Telescope Team Wins $3 Million Breakthrough Prize for Epic Black Hole Imagery."

p. 49, "World domination is not enough…" Ibid.

p. 50, "We want to make a movie…" Ibid.

p. 51, "If you study things like computer science…" "29-year-old Katie Bouman 'didn't know anything about black holes'— Then she helped capture the first photo of one."

p. 51, "There are women involved…" Sarah Mervosh, "How Katie Bouman Accidentally Became the Face of the Black Hole Project," *New York Times*, April 11, 2019, https://www.nytimes.com/2019/04/11/science/katie-bouman-black-hole.html Accessed October 23, 2019.

p. 52, "the universe has cloaked it…" Sheperd Doeleman, "Inside the black hole image that made history," TED, April 2019, https://www.ted.com/talks/sheperd_doeleman_inside_the_black_hole_image_that_made_history/transcript Accessed October 23, 2019.

p. 53, "We don't have the physics…" "Extreme Black Hole Vindicates Einstein (Again)," *National Geographic*, https://www.youtube.com/watch?v=6B3P7o8QMz8 0:25, Accessed October 23, 2019.

p. 53, "We've seen the shadow…" "Portrait of a Shadow."

Select Bibliography

Ball, Philip, "These are the discoveries that made Stephen Hawking famous." BBC, January 7, 2016, http://www.bbc.com/earth/story/20160107-these-are-the-discoveries-that-made-stephen-hawking-famous Accessed October 13, 2019.

Bouman, Katie, "How to take a picture of a black hole." *TedXBeaconStreet*, November 2016, https://www.ted.com/talks/katie_bouman_what_does_a_black_hole_look_like/transcript?language=en Accessed October 13, 2019.

Castelvecchi, Davide, "Black hole pictured for first time—in spectacular detail," *Nature*, April 10, 2019, https://www.nature.com/articles/d41586-019-01155-0 Accessed October13, 2019.

Drake, Nadia, "First-ever picture of a black hole unveiled," *National Geographic*, April 10, 2019, https://www.nationalgeographic.com/science/2019/04/first-picture-black-hole-revealed-m87-event-horizon-telescope-astrophysics/ Accessed October 13, 2019.

Fletcher, Seth. *Einstein's Shadow: A Black Hole, a Band of Astronomers, and the Quest to See the Unseeable.* New York: Ecco, 2018.

—. "How Do You Take a Picture of a Black Hole? With a Telescope as Big as the Earth." *New York Times Magazine*, October 4, 2018, https://www.nytimes.com/2018/10/04/magazine/how-do-you-take-a-picture-of-a-black-hole-with-a-telescope-as-big-as-the-earth.html Accessed October 13, 2019.

Grant, Andrew, "What it took to capture a black hole," *Physics Today*, April 11, 2019, https://physicstoday.scitation.org/do/10.1063/PT.6.1.20190411a/full/ Accessed October 13, 2019.

Greene, Jenny, "The black hole photo was no big surprise to scientists. Here's why it's still a big deal," *Washington Post*, April 12, 2019, https://www.washingtonpost.com/opinions/2019/04/12/black-hole-photo-was-no-big-surprise-scientists-heres-why-its-still-big-deal/ Accessed October 13, 2019.

Grossman, David, "How They Got the Black Hole Picture That Changed Science," *Popular Mechanics*, April 10, 2019, https://www.popularmechanics.com/space/deep-space/a27099934/eht-black-hole-picture/ Accessed October 13, 2019.

Intagliata, Christopher, "SciFri Extra: Picturing A Black Hole," *Science Friday*, April 8, 2019, https://www.sciencefriday.com/articles/picturing-a-black-hole/ Accessed October 13, 2019.

Koren, Marina, "An Extraordinary Image of the Black Hole at a Galaxy's Heart," *Atlantic*, April 10, 2019, https://www.theatlantic.com/science/archive/2019/04/black-hole-event-horizon-telescope/586846/ Accessed October 13, 2019.

Luminet, Jean-Pierre, "An Illustrated History of Black Hole Imaging: Personal Recollections (1972-2002)," [n.d..], https://arxiv.org/pdf/1902.11196.pdf Accessed October 13, 2019.

Nadis, Steve. "Why the Event Horizon Telescope took so long to image a black hole," *Astronomy*, April 10, 2019, http://www.astronomy.com/news/2019/04/the-road-to-imaging-a-black-hole Accessed October 13, 2019.

Parks, Jake, "What The Event Horizon Telescope Reveals About Galaxy M87," *Discover*, April 10, 2019, http://blogs.discovermagazine.com/crux/2019/04/10/event-horizon-telescope-galaxy-m87/#.XWxCnqjYp6w Accessed October 13, 2019.

Temming, Maria, "How scientists took the first picture of a black hole," *Science News*, April 10, 2019, https://www.sciencenews.org/article/event-horizon-telescope-black-hole-picture Accessed October 13, 2019.

Index

About the Author

Danielle Smith-Llera has written for Capstone about tiny objects and faraway targets. She welcomed this chance to write about scientists photographing one of the most mysterious objects in the universe. The power of teamwork amazes her as much as the spectacular images scientists capture—on Earth and in space.